How To Love Someone With PTSD

**The Ultimate Guide On When Someone You Love Has
And
Suffer From PTSD**

Stephanie Mike

Table of Contents

Chapter 1

Understanding PTSD

Posttraumatic Stress Disorder (PTSD) is not a new phenomenon, albeit the label is a relatively recent creation. Throughout history, dating back to the Napoleonic Wars, it has been known by a variety of names, with each successive iteration becoming progressively sterile. In 1799, "Nostalgia" was used to characterize present-day PTSD, "Soldier's Heart" following the Civil War, "Shell Shock" in World War I, "Combat Exhaustion" during WWII, "Stress Response Syndrome" post-Vietnam War, and most recently, Post Traumatic Stress Disorder.

The Diagnostic and Statistical Manual of Mental Disorders (DSM)IV defines PTSD as an anxiety disorder that can develop after a person is subjected to one or more traumatic experiences, such as sexual assault, battle, significant injury, or threats of imminent death. A diagnosis may be made when a set of symptoms, such as unsettling repeating flashbacks, avoidance or numbing of memories of the event, and hyperarousal, persist for more than a month following the traumatic event.

The individual with PTSD avoids any thoughts, emotions, and discussions about the stressor incident and may have amnesia as a result. However, the individual is frequently relieved of the experience by intrusive, recurring memories, flashbacks, and nightmares.

People deemed in danger include combat military troops, natural catastrophe victims, and victims of violent crime. People frequently sense "survivor's guilt" for living while others die. PTSD can be triggered by experiencing or witnessing a stressor event involving death, major injury, or a threat to oneself or others in a circumstance in which the individual felt tremendous fear, terror, or powerlessness.

People who work in vocations that expose them to violence, such as soldiers, or in disasters, such as emergency service workers, are also vulnerable. Because each person reacts differently to the trigger event, the most common reactions when assessing possible PTSD are vivid nightmares, alcohol and/or drug abuse, disassociation, flashback memories, and intense negative mental or physiological responses to any reminder of the traumatic event.

The Federal Veterans Affairs website estimates that there are about 21 million veterans in the United States. The conflicts in Iraq & Afghanistan are the longest combat operations since Vietnam. Many military members find that being away from home for extended periods of time causes challenges at home and at work. These issues may contribute to the stress. These are men and women who are projected to make a smooth transition back into the workforce, the majority of whom have no physical injuries.

Some studies have examined how the reaction to military stressors evolves over time. Service members were evaluated when they returned and again six months later using a simple PTSD screen. Service members were more likely to have a positive screen, which means they developed more PTSD symptoms later on. According to data, between 2002 and 2009, one million troops left active duty in Iraq or Afghanistan and became eligible for VA care. Of those servicemen, 46% sought VA services. Of those who sought VA care, 48% were diagnosed with a mental health issue. However, many Veterans who have mental health issues have not sought treatment. Veterans have stated several reasons for not receiving treatment, including:

- ❖ *They would rather rely on their friends and family.*

- ❖ *Concerns about the adverse effects of therapies.*

- ❖ *Access issues, such as treatment costs and location.*

- ❖ *Concern of being perceived as weak.*

- ❖ *Concern over being treated differently.*

- ❖ *Concern that people will lose faith in them.*

- ❖ *Concerns regarding privacy.*

It's vital to realize that not every stressful or traumatic encounter causes PTSD. Many people have unpleasant life events, such as traumatic childhoods or adult adversities, that might produce stress, anxiety, or despair but do not fulfill the definition of PTSD. Mislabeling these events as PTSD can lead to misconceptions about the disease, preventing adequate diagnosis and treatment for people who actually suffer from it.

PTSD is a serious disorder that should be recognized and understood. It is not a reaction to ordinary stress or anxiety, but rather to deeply traumatic experiences that endanger one's safety or life. Recognizing the unique nature of the trauma and symptoms associated with PTSD is critical for accurate diagnosis and treatment. By identifying PTSD from other types of mental discomfort, we can ensure that those who legitimately suffer from this condition receive the care and assistance they require.

Chapter 2

The Effects of PTSD on Relationships

How we perceive the world determines who we choose to be, and sharing compelling experiences can influence how we treat one another in positive ways. This is a powerful viewpoint.

Nothing makes you feel more powerless than living with a partner who has post-traumatic stress disorder (PTSD). I was in an intimate relationship with a man who experienced PTSD symptoms on a daily basis. My partner was a seasoned combat veteran who had served three times. The toll on his soul was awful. To escape nightmares, he became hypervigilant, feared strangers, and refused to sleep.

Being a partner to someone with PTSD can be difficult and stressful for a variety of reasons. You want to relieve their misery, but you're also grappling with your own guilt over the need to care for yourself. You want all of the answers, but you often have to accept that this is a condition that cannot be loved by someone. However, knowing the illness might help you and your partner communicate more effectively and establish healthy boundaries.

PTSD is a crippling anxiety disorder that develops following a stressful incident, such as a wartime conflict. Experts estimate that 6% of US individuals will experience PTSD to some extent over their lives. It is not something that can be overcome, like depression or other mental and behavioral difficulties. Symptoms can appear anywhere from four months to years following the triggering event. In order to be classified as PTSD, the individual must display the following characteristics:

- ❖ ***Re-experiencing symptoms such as flashbacks, nightmares, or fearful thoughts. My partner experienced awful nightmares after installing security cameras in his home to detect potential dangers.***

- ❖ *An avoidance symptom. My companion disliked crowds and avoided large-group activities.*

- ❖ *Arousal and reactivity symptoms my partner had a short fuse and became frustrated quickly when he was not understood.*

- ❖ *Cognitive and mood symptoms include low self-esteem, guilt, and blame. My boyfriend frequently asked me, why I love him because he does not see what I see in himself.*

My partner once described his PTSD to me as a perpetual waiting game for ghosts to appear around the corner. It was a reminder that horrible things had happened and that the sensation might never go away. Thunder, pyrotechnics, and truck backfiring all exacerbated the situation.

We once sat outside watching fireworks, and he held my hand until my knuckles became white, telling me that the only way he could sit through them was with me at his side. For us, these symptoms made fundamental relationship activities difficult, such as going out to dinner in a new location. Then there was the skittishness and hostility that are characteristic among those suffering from PTSD. I couldn't walk up behind him without first telling him, especially since he was wearing headphones. He also had intense spurts of fury, which made me cry.

He was the gentlest, most complimenting man 90% of the time. But when he felt injured or terrified, his nasty side took over. He knew what buttons to push, my vulnerabilities and weaknesses, and he had no shame in using them as a weapon when he was angry.

My partner is beautiful both inside and out. He is not just remarkably gorgeous, but also intelligent, considerate, and sympathetic. However, he did not believe he was deserving of love, or even remotely loveable. Traumatic experiences, in addition to scaring us and affecting our sense of safety, frequently have a direct impact on our cognitive abilities. Usually, the impacts are negative. As a result, the patient may begin to feel undeserving and unlovable, or that the world is dangerous and people cannot be trusted.

Over time, these negative beliefs grow more generalized, and negativity pervades every part of life. They may also carry over into a relationship. My partner frequently asked me what I saw in him and how I could love him. This underlying insecurity influenced how I handled him, providing extra reassurance without urging.

My spouse required a great deal of time and attention from me. Because he had lost so much in his life, he had an almost controlling grasp on me, from demanding to know every detail of my movements and having meltdowns when the plan changed at the last minute, to wanting me to be loyal to him over my own parents, even when I thought he didn't always deserve it.

But I obliged him. I walked out of the room with some pals and talked on the phone with him for hours. I took images of someone I was with to show him I wasn't cheating or leaving him. I choose him over everyone in my life. Because I figured that if I didn't, who would? My partner's belief that he was unlovable led him to invent settings that portrayed him as such. When he was enraged, he would take vicious punches at me. I'd be torn apart, concerned about the next time my partner tried to verbally attack me. At the same time, he sometimes did not feel comfortable opening up to me, which was another indicator of his PTSD.

I've encountered lots of cases in which the partner is unaware that their significant other is suffering from PTSD. All they sense is rage from their partner, however, in truth, this person has psychological harm and is suffering but does not know how to communicate it. This leads to increasing disconnection within the relationship, resulting in a vicious cycle.

People suffering from PTSD have options despite their feelings of hopelessness and loneliness. The best way to deal with mental health issues is to educate yourself and seek professional help. People with PTSD believe they are going insane and are completely alone in their state. The partner feels the same way.

Many people who are in relationships with someone who has PTSD take on the role of caretaker. At least this was the case for me, I wanted to be the one who didn't desert my partner; I wanted to show him that love can overcome all obstacles and, with the proper person, can help him reinforce and reestablish a healthy lifestyle.

As heartbreaking as it is to admit, love does not always win out. This realization came in waves over the years we were together, accompanied by strong feelings of remorse and inadequacy. The idea that we can save people is an illusion. It is ultimately their responsibility as adults to seek or ask for treatment, even if the trauma they encountered was not their fault. We can't make anyone take aid.

Caregivers in interactions with people suffering from PTSD frequently neglect their own well-being. Because it is so simple to get into an unhealthy pattern, I acquired guilt connected with personal fulfillment or satisfaction. I felt bad because I wanted to hang out with friends without having to spend an hour chatting down with my boyfriend or not checking in on a regular basis when traveling for work to let him know I was safe.

The companion of someone with PTSD will need to be strong most of the time. To accomplish this, you must first prioritize your own mental health. When you are a caretaker, you must first put on your own mask. Making time for oneself requires a conscious effort. The caretaker must remain strong in order to become a support system, and they must have help and healthy outlets to do so.

Chapter 3

Creating a Supportive Environment

If your partner has PTSD, you may be at a loss for how to help them deal with the disorder's unpleasant symptoms.

Understand PTSD

PTSD can cause people to behave irrationally or inexplicably. They may retreat emotionally, become angry or paranoid, or behave in a volatile or unpredictable manner. Their loved ones are frequently annoyed and perplexed by their behavior, and they may even begin to exhibit trauma symptoms themselves. It can be important to remember that your partner may not fully understand their behavior, so give them the benefit of the doubt to foster a supportive environment.

Actively Listen

Trauma is difficult to discuss, so don't force your partner to open up. This can backfire, making healing even more difficult. Let your spouse know that you are available to talk about it if they want, but they are not required to. Be patient so that your partner can gradually become comfortable talking openly about the painful incident. When they are able to open up, offer them your whole attention, listen without judgment, and avoid giving them advice.

Help Them Socialize

People who have PTSD are more likely to suffer from social anxiety disorder. People with PTSD frequently feel the desire to withdraw from others, which can lead to feelings of isolation from the outside world. They may also lose interest in their activities and avoid social interactions. This isn't because they don't care; rather, they're in pain. While you should respect your partner's boundaries, gently encourage them to partake in social activities and hobbies that they enjoy. Social connection is an important component of healing, so try to assist your spouse stay connected.

Support Their Treatment

People with PTSD should seek treatment. Encourage them to seek treatment and utilize other self-care strategies to manage. Help them find a therapist who specializes in trauma and can assist them with specific therapy strategies. For example, cognitive behavioral therapy has been demonstrated to be useful in the treatment of PTSD. In addition, they may benefit from breathing exercises, meditation, yoga, or support groups. Whatever works best for them, be sure to support and encourage them.

Be Secure and Trustworthy

When a person is traumatized, they lose the ability to trust others and themselves. They may constantly feel insecure in this world. You may aid children by making your connection a secure and dependable shelter for them. Keeping your vows, remaining dedicated to the relationship, and making future plans that incorporate them can all help your spouse feel more comfortable.

Recognize Their Trigger

Recognizing your triggers, or the items that produce pain and flashbacks, is an important step in the recovery process for PTSD. This could be specific places, images, sounds, or situations. Knowing your partner's triggers and devising a strategy for dealing with them might help them develop coping skills for these situations.

Being in a relationship with someone who has PTSD is not always easy, but learning about the disease can help you meet them where they are.

Chapter 4

Effective Communication Strategies

People are generally programmed to listen with ulterior motives in mind, whether to persuade, judge, or create an impression. We frequently listen for self-serving reasons. How often do we listen solely for the purpose of listening? Because of what they are going through, loved ones with PTSD are especially sensitive to our intentions. In their minds, individuals may believe that no one understands what is going on in their heads and that everyone is merely trying to give them useless advice.

One of the most powerful methods to connect with someone who has been traumatized is to simply listen: to comprehend, sympathize with, and record what your loved one is going through. Listening without disguised objectives allows people to be vulnerable and seek help.

Once people have expressed their views and feelings, it can be beneficial to inquire about trigger management. Certain stimuli, such as a traumatic event, sight, sound, smell, or other things, might trigger PTSD. It might be really helpful to ask individuals how you can help them manage these stresses.

Sometimes it's more than just avoiding triggers; it's also about assisting folks in dealing with and responding to unexpected stimuli. Other ways to show your support during hardships and triggers include:

- ❖ *Expressing that you are willing to listen.*
- ❖ *Reminding people of prospective circumstances in which they may encounter triggers.*
- ❖ *Informing people ahead of time about potential triggers.*
- ❖ *Helping people find strategies to relax in situations that may be causing flashbacks or other symptoms of stress.*

Being aware of your loved one's triggers can improve how they deal with PTSD.

Give folks options to start finding aid

You don't want to compel individuals to seek help. When people are motivated to treat a dual diagnosis or a disease that combines both a mental disorder, such as PTSD, and an alcohol or drug addiction, it is easier and more effective.

If your loved one is unsure about seeking help, don't force your views right immediately. Instead, provide options and explain how they can help. Allow people to choose what they believe will work for them, such as seeking therapy, going to rehab, or getting a doctor's checkup first. Giving your loved ones the space and freedom to choose might help them feel more in control of their actions, paving the way for self-motivation.

It's one thing to applaud your loved one's success in quitting drinking or finding work after rehab--these are excellent successes. However, it may be extremely beneficial to recognize their modest triumphs, such as spending more time socializing with others, venturing beyond their comfort zones, or dealing with a difficult circumstance well.

Expressing to them that they are on the right track and demonstrating that you perceive them and their accomplishments are two ways you may genuinely boost your loved one and help them manage PTSD. You can be proud of supporting and encouraging your partner who has PTSD. While navigating PTSD can be difficult, implementing a few tactics can help your loved one move closer to recovery.

Avoiding Triggers in Conversations

First and foremost, be present and kind throughout all attempts to repair and deepen a relationship. The intensity of others' emotions is impossible to comprehend or fully evaluate, thus a figurative soft touch will suffice.

The methods of dealing with trauma vary according to the sufferer's experiences and personality. There is no universal solution that works for everyone, but some ways are more likely to be effective than others. Whether you're in problems yourself or in a relationship with someone who is, the strategy to alleviate the strain is similar.

Open communication is the foundation of any effective relationship, including how we interact with ourselves. Any partnership that does not make a concerted effort to maintain open communication between its members is doomed to collapse. Consider what excellent communication is, which is a great place to start, especially when dealing with possible triggers that must be recognized in order to be addressed effectively.

Good communication enables both parties in a relationship to provide the framework for investigating why certain events may elicit a rapid negative reaction. Emotions frequently do not appear reasonable until their cause is identified, but this does not imply that the reaction is wholly irrational. Taking the time and effort to identify the source of the trigger sheds insight into the problem, making it much easier to assess and hence alleviate.

Communication is presenting your thoughts and emotions clearly and truthfully, as well as paying close attention to what others are saying. This may appear straightforward on paper, but we are often a lot more stubborn than we would want to acknowledge. It is extremely simple to exchange a painful truth for a convenient innocuous falsehood, for example.

While it is understandable not to always tell the truth for the purpose of convenience, lying is a major impediment to clear and meaningful communication. Before dealing with trauma-related triggers, both persons in the relationship must agree on a common aim. The shared goal in this scenario should be to communicate the absolute truth, with the awareness that anything less is detrimental to true communication and so cannot be utilized as a tool to tackle any of the issues at hand.

Once this is determined and agreed upon, you have successfully laid the groundwork for future development. The debate becomes easier when no mistrust, second-guessing, or delusions are involved. If you don't keep your cool, relationship discussions might lead to conflicts or rivalry. Remembering that you are a team and that your goals are aligned is also critical before attempting to address any sensitive topic that is generating relationship problems.

Understanding a problem is necessary before we can fix it. The first step toward achieving this goal is to discuss the issue and how it affects the relationship. This is no easy task, as it may seem like perilous territory to enter. If engaging in conversation about a particular topic seems risky, it's probably best to avoid it. As a rule of thumb, unresolved traumatic situations tend to fester in the sufferer's psyche rather than improve with time. If you can gently pull them out of their shell, that will be a tremendous win on their path to recovery.

While discussing the issue may feel like poking your hand in a fire, pointing out the consequences of a previous triggering event is not the same as forcing your loved one to relive their pain all over again. That is, raising the issue will not always elicit a response, even if it appears risky. Finally, the first step is the most difficult, and everything else will become simpler from here.

Walking on eggshells is a bad way to spend your life and will eventually wear you down. There's a lot to be said about confronting a problem directly, especially when the alternative is a steady spiral into never-ending agony. Avoiding the issue at hand will do nothing to improve the relationship. Pick your words wisely and show that you're willing to assist. While a dug-up land mine may still explode, at least it is above ground and you know where not to step. Unearthing the problem will prepare you both to deal with it jointly.

You might or might not know the trigger if you're the partner of someone who struggles with mental illness. It's frightening to see a loved one suddenly, and sometimes for no apparent reason, begin to suffer intense and crippling emotions. Without a clear cause, you may feel helpless and bewildered while your partner's attention shifts inward to protect themselves.

They may also become irritable, accusing, or violent. Regardless of their external look, it will be evident that they are experiencing great mental conflict. It is also normal for the suffering to block all attempts to contact them while fighting a struggle that only they are aware of. How you react is critical, and it's impossible to know how to assist without first discussing what to do when it happens. Your first instinct might be to embrace them, for example, and console them as best you can. Depending on the extent of their trauma, it's easy to see why this could be a mistake, despite your best intentions.

This is one of the reasons why communication is so vital, and it's worth laying your cards on the table in order to establish some coping methods. This allows for conversation about strategy in the event of the worst-case scenario, allowing you to know how to best support your loved one without making matters worse. Knowing you have a strategy in place can also assist in reducing tension in the relationship and make the sufferer feel seen, understood, and supported, easing much of their concern about prospective relapses.

If feasible, ask your partner to talk about their terrible experiences. This will most likely be difficult for them, but explain that if you had a better understanding of the source of their misery, you'd be better able to avoid doing or doing anything that could provoke an episode. Armed with a deeper grasp of the underlying issue, you may be able to avoid triggering their trauma entirely.

If going into the basis of the problem is too much for your partner, ask them to tell you what to avoid. Actions and statements that appear benign to you may provoke a painful memory. Of course, not all triggers come from without, but you might try to avoid being the source of specific external triggers.

Internal triggers are more difficult to deal with because they are completely beyond your control. Unwanted thoughts of the PTSD sufferer might arise at any time and send them into a downward spiral, even if the day is going well. If possible, distinguish between the two.

A helpful method, for example, is for the sufferer to clarify that the cause isn't their partner or something they've done if they're having an internal episode. This will assist the sufferer's spouse in understanding how to effectively assist them without feeling guilty, while also providing the sufferer with a manner of secure pre-agreed upon support. With a few tools in place, dealing with trauma triggers in relationships becomes much easier. The initial discussions may be painful, but the structure gained as a result is well worth it.

Managing Flashbacks

Flashbacks are vivid experiences in which a person recalls details of a traumatic event. It can be difficult to know how to aid during a flashback, but you do not need specific expertise to assist someone who is experiencing one. It may help if you:

- ❖ *Avoid making quick movements.*
- ❖ *Encourage them to breathe slowly and deeply.*
- ❖ *Encourage them to explain their environment.*
- ❖ *Try to remain calm.*
- ❖ *Gently inform them that they are experiencing a flashback.*

Chapter 5

Encourage Professional Help

Getting your partner treated for PTSD might be beneficial for them, but therapy may also help you cope with the changes in your relationship. Several evidence-based, trauma-focused therapies are effective for your partner's PTSD. If you or your partner are unsure how to find a therapist, requesting a reference from your health care practitioner or using an internet therapy directory are excellent ways to begin. Three types of therapy are thought to be the most successful in treating PTSD:

Eye movement desensitization and reprocessing therapy (EMDR)
EMDR is a highly effective treatment for PTSD. It can help your partner process trauma and reduce extreme reactions to stimuli. These sessions are often held once or twice a week for 6-12 hours, with each session lasting 60-90 minutes in person or online.

Cognitive Process Therapy (CPT)
CPT assists your spouse in identifying and changing negative thoughts, which frequently accompany the beginning of PTSD. During CPT sessions, your spouse will work with the therapist to uncover negative beliefs caused by the traumatic experience and then challenge them with healthier, more positive ones.

Prolonged Exposure (PE)
PE largely addresses the avoidance part of trauma. The reminders of traumatic experiences that your partner wishes to avoid are confronted front on by continuously discussing and thereby exposing them to the traumatic memories in a safe setting. The goal is to recover control of your partner's thoughts and feelings so that they can improve their quality of life.

Couples' Therapy Options

If you and your spouse want to go to therapy together, the most extensively researched and well-known type of couples counseling where one person has PTSD is cognitive-behavioral conjoint therapy (CBCT). It was specifically intended to reduce PTSD symptoms and promote relationship adjustment using a cognitive-behavioral, interpersonal understanding of PTSD.

According to this idea, cognitive, behavioral, and affective processes all interact to affect the individual and their spouse, resulting in the maintenance of PTSD symptoms and relational issues. CBCT focuses on themes in your relationship and emphasizes communicating thoughts and feelings. It comprises fifteen 75-minute sessions and seeks to make sense of the traumatic event.

How to Encourage Therapy Participation

What happens now that your spouse or loved one is in therapy? Here are some methods to help your partner in treatment.

Respect their privacy

There are numerous positive features to therapy, one of which is confidentiality. The therapist's confidentiality is required, strictly guarded, and crucial. For the person in therapy, having the security to process ideas and feelings in a safe environment may be a profoundly healing experience.

Therefore, it is crucial to respect your partner's privacy. Your partner has opted to get therapy, which is a deeply personal decision. This practice can be upsetting, tiring, and difficult to express or discuss outside of sessions. However, your spouse may choose to speak with you about their sessions. If this is the case, it may be beneficial to address your partner's level of comfort with what and how they want to disclose. Establish ground rules for these preferences.

Respect your partner's confidence by refraining from disclosing sensitive information to outsiders. Allow your partner the space they require, and realize that this is their job and experience. You have a supporting role.

Become interested

Therapy can be a difficult, emotional process. Your partner may continue to process themes, emotions, or experiences discussed during sessions. They may wish to discuss facts they have discovered or new insights they have had. Your partner may wish to talk about behavioral patterns or lessons learned. Alternatively, they may be fatigued and seek a break from the hard emotional lifting done in treatment, preferring space or a new activity.

Another area where your spouse may need assistance is with homework assignments that demand your participation. If that's the case, making yourself available and willing to get involved in the homework exercises is critical. If you are unsure about your partner's needs, ask them. Keep in mind that their support needs may change between sessions. Check in with your partner to see what they need and how you can best support them.

Keep in mind that you are not responsible for acting as a therapist, simply provide them the opportunity to share.

Maintain reasonable expectations

Therapy does not provide rapid results or magical solutions. Be patient. Respect your partner's experience and do not anticipate fast results. Just because your partner is in therapy does not indicate that changes will occur overnight. Understand that the therapeutic journey is not a straight line, but rather a road with bends, bumps, dips, and ditches that necessitate grace, honesty, and patience.

Remember that just because your partner is in treatment does not mean that all of your relationship issues will be resolved. In truth, it may be beneficial to evaluate how you and your partner could benefit from your own therapy.

Relationships necessitate that each person recognize, accept, and address their own weaknesses. And it may feel like a huge weight to assist your partner in their therapy journey. You are not expected to bear the additional burden alone. If your emotional support system is weak or you would benefit from having a neutral third party, hiring your own therapist may assist you in handling any emotional weight while supporting your partner.

Offer encouragement

Therapy can be difficult, exhausting work, and your partner may feel overwhelmed by a range of feelings. Offering your spouse encouragement during their therapy journey may give them reassurance, inspiration, or motivation.

Recognize your partner's bravery in getting assistance and their willingness to be vulnerable throughout therapy. Your partner may even begin to practice new abilities, ways of being, or reacting to you in your relationship. This can seem reckless and raw. Offer your partner grace and support while they try something new. Encouraging your spouse may help them stay motivated and gain confidence as they work toward the goals they set in treatment.

Celebrates

Celebrate the significant progress your spouse achieves toward growth and healing. Celebrate both the little, seemingly unimportant changes and your partner's commitment to therapy.

It's easy to ignore victories, but now is the moment to recognize change and growth. Celebrate your partner's efforts and investment in healing, their hard work, and the results of their therapeutic journey.

Some people may recover rapidly, such as within a year, whilst others may acquire chronic PTSD, necessitating regular and watchful monitoring as well as a good treatment plan to allow the patient to live a normal life despite suffering from this mental illness. The best method to assist your spouse with suspected PTSD is to have them receive a formal diagnosis from a GP or Psychiatrist so that they can develop a treatment plan that should be reviewed with the treating professional.

Chapter 6

Self-Care for Partners

Some partners go through hoops in an attempt to help their spouse, only to feel alone, disappointed, and inept when their partner does not respond as they would like. Without additional self-care, a trauma survivor's spouse may experience burnout in general, as well as burnout in the relationship. To ensure your own mental health and be able to best serve your partner, partners must learn to care for themselves.

Identify your triggers in relation to your partner's trauma
Based on what you know about your partner's traumatic experience and how you reacted to hearing about it, you will most likely find particular people, places, or things unpleasant or triggering, just as someone with PTSD might. For example, a combat veteran's wife may find watching TV coverage of the conflict anxiety-inducing after learning her spouse was injured in an IED.

Just like a trauma survivor, it is OK in the near term to limit your exposure to people, places, or things that you find triggering. This will allow you to conserve your emotional energy and better regulate your feelings about what transpired. Triggers can't all be avoided. When you experience a reaction to a trigger, be patient and understanding with yourself.

Do not invalidate your own experiences of what happened
Many partners of trauma survivors blame themselves for their own reactions to their partner's suffering. They believe that because they were not the ones who experienced the trauma, they should be able to cope with it. This proposal is unrealistic. Your partner's trauma will have an effect on you to some extent, and you must identify your own reaction to it in order to heal and assist your partner effectively.

Increase your social support

To deal with the trauma or PTSD symptoms, your partner may withdraw from others [hyperlink]. In your efforts to help your partner and deal with your own trauma, you may find yourself withdrawing from others. Be careful not to isolate yourself, since you will require the assistance of understanding family members and friends to deal with this predicament. In addition to trauma support, your friends and family can help you keep some sense of normalcy in your life.

Develop a realistic life plan

The trauma, and how each of you deals with it, will have an impact on your short-term and long-term life plans, depending on how severe it is. To be fair to yourself, your spouse, and the relationship, you must alter your life plan to reflect the current circumstances. You must select what is negotiable and how long. Only you can determine what you are willing to adjust and change.

Establish appropriate boundaries with your partner

Your partner will most likely rely on you more while they deal with the consequences of the tragedy. However, you do have wants and restrictions. If you don't set boundaries with your partner about how you can help, you'll burn out and respond passive-aggressively. If you overgive, you will grow resentful and furious with your partner. You must know what you can give and then give freely.

At the end of the day, you will not be able to meet all of your partner's requirements, which is fine. They will be frustrated that you are unable to satisfy more of your wants, but this is acceptable. If you set proper limitations for what you can give, your partner will gradually come to value what you can give. You also need to give your spouse permission to feel upset with you and accept that this is normal. Remember that, while you can assist your spouse in recovering, you are not responsible for their recovery. Ultimately, your partner is responsible for his or her own healing.

Be realistic about your partner's healing

It is unfair to your partner and your relationship to have unreasonable expectations about what healing should look like and how quickly it should happen. The reality is that the process differs for each trauma survivor. Even if your partner no longer matches the criteria for full-blown PTSD, various life events and scenarios will always trigger some PTSD symptoms in him/her.

The main thing is for you and your partner to communicate properly when you have opposing views on how and what mending should look like. When conflict emerges, seeking treatment from a therapist may be beneficial. This is why you established boundaries so that if their healing takes longer than expected, you would be able to cope.

Know when to seek professional help
You, like your partner, may require professional assistance in recovering from the trauma! At The Center for Growth, we can assist trauma survivors' partners in dealing with their own trauma-related emotions. Just because you did not personally experience the trauma does not mean that you will be unaffected by it. The trauma will have an influence on you in some form, and you may require individual therapy at some point.

- *Deal with your own trauma-related reactions.*
- *Deal with your reaction to your partner dealing with a trauma victim.*
- *Handle the symptoms of secondary trauma reactions, which resemble PTSD symptoms.*
- *Improve your understanding of PTSD and the healing process after trauma.*
- *Make your own judgment on whether or not to stay in the relationship.*

Partners of trauma survivors must adjust to the new reality caused by their partner's trauma. Creating healthy boundaries with their partner and engaging in self-care is essential for partners of trauma survivors to prevent burnout and provide effective support to their partners.

Conclusion

Dating someone with post-traumatic stress disorder (PTSD) can be a unique experience in the realm of PTSD dating, full of challenges and potential for growth. Understanding the complexity of PTSD and how it affects relationships is critical to developing a supportive and empathetic connection.

Post-Traumatic Stress Disorder (PTSD) is a mental health illness caused by a traumatic incident, whether experienced or witnessed. It is a reaction to severe trauma, such as armed conflict, natural disasters, terrorist attacks, serious accidents, or violent personal assaults. PTSD affects everyone differently, and its effects can be far-reaching, affecting not just those who suffer from it, but also those closest to them.

PTSD symptoms are typically classified into four types: intrusive memories, such as flashbacks and nightmares; aversion to reminders of the trauma; negative changes in thoughts and mood, such as feelings of emptiness and emotional numbness; and heightened reactions, such as irritability or being easily startled. Dating someone who has PTSD due to narcissistic abuse might be more difficult since this type of trauma damages interpersonal relationships and trust in particular ways. So, while dating someone with PTSD, expect mood swings and emotional instability.

Expectations for Dating Someone With PTSD

When dating someone with Post-Traumatic Stress Disorder (PTSD), keep in mind that their worldview may differ from that of someone without PTSD. Trauma from the past might have an impact on their behavior and feelings today. Here are seven things to expect in such a relationship:

Diverse emotional responses
Your partner may experience a wide range of emotions as a result of their PTSD. They may experience unexpected mood changes,

strong anger, despair, or terror that appear disproportionate to the situation. These emotional responses are frequently linked to past traumatic experiences that have had a significant impact on their psyche. Understanding and patience are essential for negotiating these periods.

Withdrawal and isolation

Individuals with PTSD may frequently withdraw into themselves, especially when they are feeling overwhelmed. Your lover may shun social gatherings and private moments with you. Such seclusion is a coping mechanism for potential triggers or overpowering emotions, not a reflection of their sentiments for you.

Communication challenges

Someone suffering from PTSD may find it exceedingly difficult to talk about their feelings or painful experiences. They may find it difficult to express their emotions or avoid discussing their past. Respecting their pace and comfort zone while encouraging open conversation within safe bounds is critical.

Hyperarousal

Being constantly attentive is frequent with PTSD. Your partner might react strongly to sudden occurrences, loud noises, or fast movements.They may also experience difficulties relaxing or sleeping. This heightened level of anxiety is caused by their brain being always on the alert for danger, a residual effect of their traumatic experiences.

Flashbacks and triggers

Flashbacks are situations where your partner relives an experience due to specific odors, noises, places, or even persons. During these instances, they may lose touch with reality, resulting in distress and perplexity. It is imperative to comprehend their triggers and help them become grounded in the here and now.

Intimacy difficulties

PTSD can have a severe impact on both physical and emotional intimacy. Your spouse may have periods when they are distant or uninterested in sexual activity. Traumatic incidents, particularly those involving physical or emotional abuse, might complicate intimacy. Building trust and communicating clearly about comfort levels and boundaries is critical.

Need for space

There will be times when your partner requires space to process their feelings or deal with their symptoms. This need for solitude is not a rejection, but rather part of their coping method. Respecting their desire for distance while letting them know you're accessible when they're ready to reconnect is critical to a good relationship.

Ways to support your partner who has PTSD

Understanding, patience, and a willingness to adjust to your partner's specific requirements are required when supporting someone with PTSD. It's about creating a safe and trusting environment in which they can continue their healing journey with your help. So, here are methods to aid a partner with PTSD:

Educate yourself on PTSD

Take the time to understand your partner's PTSD, including the symptoms and how it affects them. This information will assist you in understanding your partner's behavior and emotions. Living with someone who has PTSD requires being aware of what they are going through and how to best support them.

Practice active listening

Listen attentively to your spouse without attempting to solve their concerns right away. Sometimes all they want is to be understood and heard. Active listening entails being present, expressing empathy, and acknowledging their experiences without judgment.

Encourage professional help

Encourage your partner to get therapy or counseling. PTSD is a complex condition that frequently necessitates professional attention.

Encourage them gently, but do not force the topic. Professional assistance might be critical in managing PTSD symptoms.

Establish a safe environment
Creating a safe and predictable setting can assist in reducing anxiety and hyperarousal symptoms. This could include setting routines or making the home a quiet and secure environment. Remember that safety is both physical and mental.

Respect their triggers
Be aware of any settings, conversations, or occurrences that may trigger your partner's PTSD symptoms. Avoiding these triggers, or preparing for them when avoidance is unavoidable, is an essential component of PTSD partner support.

Support their healing path
Be patient as your companion heals. Understand that recovery is not a linear process with ups and downs. Show empathy and support throughout their journey, celebrating little accomplishments and providing consolation during setbacks.

Communicate frankly and honestly
Good communication is essential in any healthy relationship, but it is especially important in a connection with someone with PTSD. Encourage honest and open conversation, ensuring that both of you feel comfortable expressing your opinions and feelings.

Take care of yourself
Making your own mental and emotional health a priority is essential. Ascertain that you have a support network and engage in self-care. This is critical to your capacity to remain a helpful partner.

Be patient and sympathetic
Your partner may experience trouble or relapse into terrible recollections, and during these moments, patience and compassion are essential. Recognize that healing takes time and that your steadfast support can be a vital tool in their recovery.